AN ABBEVILLE ANTHOLOGY

# Stories
## from the
# Sea

Compiled by James Riordan
Illustrated by Amanda Hall

First published in Great Britain in 1996 by Barefoot Books Ltd.
First published in the United States of America in 1996 by Abbeville Press,
488 Madison Avenue, New York, N.Y. 10022.

This book has been printed on 100% acid-free paper

Page layouts: Amanda Hall
Graphic design: Design/Section
Printed and bound in Hong Kong

First edition
10 9 8 7 6 5 4 3 2 1

ISBN 0-7892-0282-4

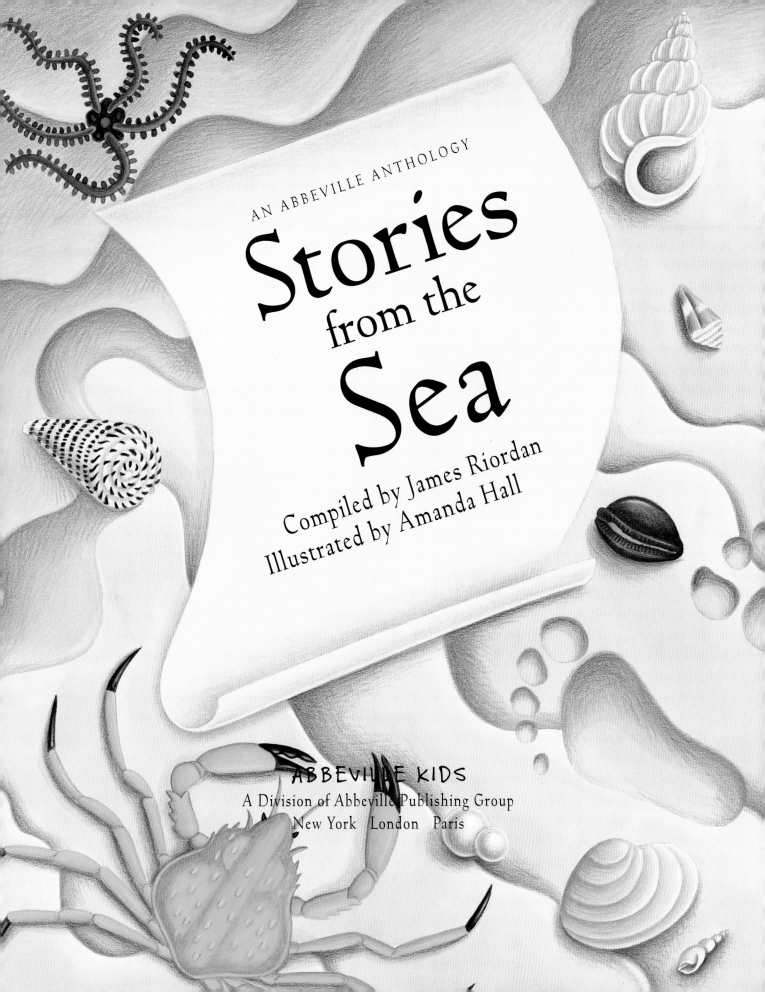

AN ABBEVILLE ANTHOLOGY

# Stories
## from the
# Sea

Compiled by James Riordan
Illustrated by Amanda Hall

ABBEVILLE KIDS
A Division of Abbeville Publishing Group
New York  London  Paris

# Contents

# *Foreword*

*T*his collection of tales from around the world is set in and around the sea. Some stories are well known, like Hans Christian Andersen's "The Little Mermaid" and the Arabian "Sinbad the Sailor" from "The Thousand and One Nights." Some—such as "The Flood" and "Why the Sea is Salty"—pose age-old questions; others cast up a variety of good and evil sea spirits—mermaids, sea gods and selkies.

These stories of the sea cross vast oceans—the Indian Ocean ("Sinbad the Sailor"), the Arctic Ocean ("The Old Man of the Sea"), the Pacific ("The Precious Pearl"), and the Atlantic ("The Flood"); they wash into mighty seas like the Baltic off the coasts of Denmark and Finland ("The Little Mermaid" and "Why the Sea is Salty"), and the North Sea that surrounds the Orkneys ("The Selkie Wife"); they course into river mouths off the west coast of Africa ("Sea Wind") and even into New Zealand's Lake Rotorua, not far from the Bay of Plenty ("Hine-moa").

The sea seems to hold a special place in all cultures; for many peoples there is no other feature of nature that they so vividly depict in their tales. And for good reason: the sea, with its sheer power and unpredictable moods, has always inspired both fear and deep affection. It can be hugely destructive, yet men and women have placed their homes upon its shores and been fed by it; for the merchant it has been the means to reach other lands, to trade goods and experience, to invent and adapt new forms of ocean-going craft; and it has brought nations together, making them feel part of the greater world, and teaching them respect for the customs of other people.

The sea has always had its great mysteries too. Even today it is easy to believe that the spirit of the sea murmurs and glistens when contented, or roars and seethes when angry. The constant motion of water, accompanied by changing weather patterns, naturally suggests that the sea is alive. So for our ancestors the sea, and its sons and daughters—the rivers and lakes—all had their evil or helpful spirits. It may be an old, green-bearded sea giant who, when drunk, makes the waters overflow. When pleased, he guides the fish into fishermen's nets. When angry, he raises storms, sinks ships, seizes and strangles sailors, tears traps and lines. In the depths of the water live other spirits: the mermaids, water nymphs or selkies, lovely naked women with skins the color of moonlight, silken hair and emerald eyes. Often, they so charm passers-by with their song and laughter that men drown themselves for their sake.

These stories conjure up a host of spirits and creatures in different shapes and forms, but all the tales are linked by an awe of and respect for the sea's wonderful, magical power—a feeling which is shared by people the world over.

*James Riordan*

# The Flood

NATIVE AMERICAN

Once upon a time, in the land that is now called North America, it started to rain. The mountain streams were swollen, the rivers choked, and the sea began to rise.

Still it rained. For weeks and weeks, the mountain torrents thundered down, and the sea crept silently up. The lowlands were the first to disappear. Next the sloping hills slipped into the sea. The whole world was slowly being swallowed up by the Flood.

Hurriedly, many tribes gathered in one spot, a place of safety far above the sea. They held a council to decide upon a plan. After the elders had talked together for many hours, one of them announced: "We shall build a great canoe and anchor it to a rock until the waters die down. The men

7

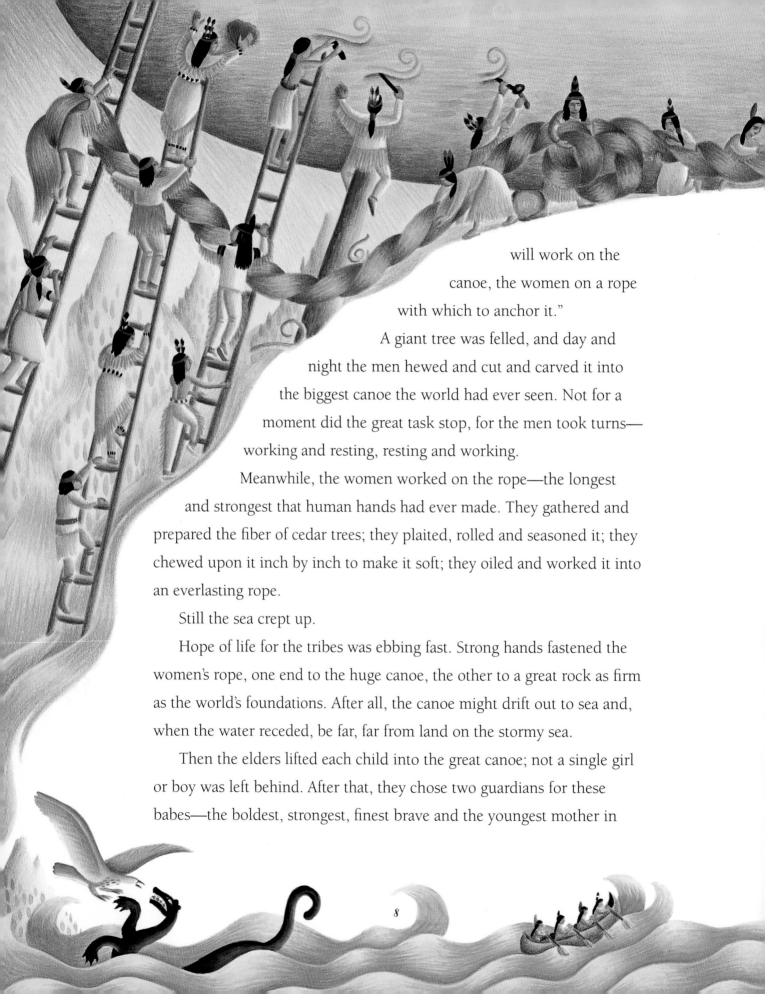

will work on the
canoe, the women on a rope
with which to anchor it."

A giant tree was felled, and day and
night the men hewed and cut and carved it into
the biggest canoe the world had ever seen. Not for a
moment did the great task stop, for the men took turns—
working and resting, resting and working.

Meanwhile, the women worked on the rope—the longest
and strongest that human hands had ever made. They gathered and
prepared the fiber of cedar trees; they plaited, rolled and seasoned it; they
chewed upon it inch by inch to make it soft; they oiled and worked it into
an everlasting rope.

Still the sea crept up.

Hope of life for the tribes was ebbing fast. Strong hands fastened the
women's rope, one end to the huge canoe, the other to a great rock as firm
as the world's foundations. After all, the canoe might drift out to sea and,
when the water receded, be far, far from land on the stormy sea.

Then the elders lifted each child into the great canoe; not a single girl
or boy was left behind. After that, they chose two guardians for these
babes—the boldest, strongest, finest brave and the youngest mother in

any of the
tribes. The woman was to
sit at the bow to keep watch, the
brave at the stern to guide the boat, with
all the children in between.

And still the sea crept up.

At the crest of a bluff above the sea, the doomed
tribes crowded round; no one tried to join the great canoe;
no one cried or wailed over their fate.

"Let the children, the young mother, and the strong brave live
on," they prayed as the waters rose above their heads.

And still the sea crept up. After the top of the tallest pine had
disappeared, all was a world of sea. The canoe rose up with the water and
floated on the waves.

For days and days, there was no land—just a rush of swirling,
snarling sea. But the canoe rode safely at anchor, the women's rope held
true, as true as the hearts that beat behind the labor of it all.

One morning at sunrise, a tiny speck was seen floating on the sea's
green surface, far to the south. At midday it grew larger; by evening it was
bigger still. The moon rose and in its pale light the young woman saw that
the speck was a patch of land. All night she watched it grow, and at

daybreak she looked with happy eyes upon the summit of what is now called Mount Baker, in British Columbia.

The young brave cut the rope, grasped the paddle in his strong hands

and steered south. By the time the canoe finally ran ashore, the waters had
rolled halfway down the mountainside. The children were lifted out, the
young mother and the brave turned to each other, clasped hands, looked

into each other's eyes, and smiled.

And down in the vast land that lies between Mount Baker and the Fraser River they built new homes where the little children lived and grew up, and life was renewed.

It is said that in a crevice halfway up Mount Baker the outlines of a huge canoe may still be seen, so the memory of its builders will never fade.

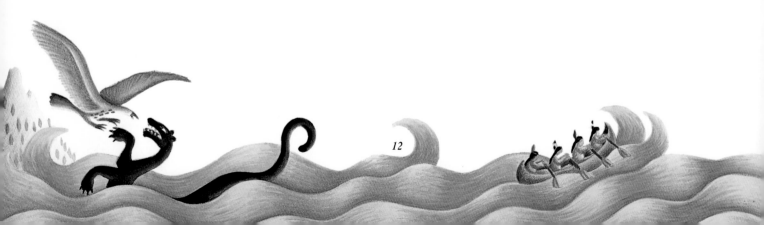

# The Selkie Wife

CELTIC

It is said by those who know that seals were once humans who drowned in the sea. Now only their wise, soft, loving eyes betray their human past. Yet sometimes, when no one is around, they come ashore, cast off their animal skins, and dance upon the sand.

There was once a cottage that stood by itself upon a cliff, and this cottage was the home of a lonely fisherman. Although he fished and laid traps until the tiredness in his bones drove the dreams away, there were times when loneliness made his eyes overflow and rivers of tears coursed down his cheeks.

One evening in late summer, the fisherman was sitting on a rock, his chin cupped in his hands, gazing out to sea. The distant sunset gave out a rich glow and the calm sea gleamed pink and gold. All at once, he caught snatches of song and laughter coming from the seaward side of the rocks at the far end of the shore.

Creeping forwards, he crossed the sand, climbed up the rocks, and peered over the other side. There below him by the water's edge in a sheltered inlet was a ring of women dancing, singing—all as naked as the sun-splashed rocks. Never in all his years had he seen such lovely faces, such graceful limbs, such smooth skins the color of moonlight.

"Aye, I know you," he murmured to himself. "Selkies! And what if I should take a wild wee skin for myself?"

With these words he scrambled back down the rocks, ran across the sand, and snatched up a silvery skin before they saw him.

When they finally noticed the man, each selkie made a dash to seize her skin, crying and yelping like seal cubs at dawn. Then, diving into the sea, they swam swiftly away, pulling on their seal skins as they went.

Meanwhile the fisherman was making off with the selkie skin under his arm. But before he reached the cliff path, he heard soft footsteps padding quickly after him and the sound of someone weeping. As he turned, he saw a woman holding out her arms to him.

"Wait, sir," she cried. "Give me back my selkie skin!"

The moon shone upon her naked form and two big crystal tears rolled down her cheeks. The fisherman thought she was the loveliest woman he had ever seen.

"You'll not be away to sea again," he said. "You'll stay with me and be my good wife."

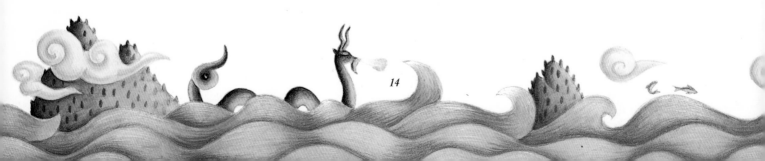

"But I cannot be that," she said. "I'm not yours to take. I am of another folk."

"If you become my wife," the fisherman continued, "I'll return your selkie skin in seven years to the day."

It seemed she had no choice.

The fisherman put his plaid cloak about the woman and led her home to his cottage. There he wrapped her in a blanket and gave her supper—round, flat *bannock* cakes and hot *brose,* or porridge. While she was eating, he stole out to the barn, folded up the skin, and hid it on a beam beneath the roof.

In the course of time she had a child; there was no bonnier boy in all the isle—he had large, gentle eyes and smooth brown skin.

How he loved his mother: he would rub his cheek against hers, inhale the odor of her skin, caress her long brown hair. Smiling, she would show him three suede pouches that she had sewn herself—one full of berries, one of dried flowers, one of little stones and shells. Then she would press her palm to the sandy earth and say, "What is there?"

"Nothing. What could there be?" he'd reply.

With a little laugh, she would raise her hand. And there upon the soil were spread pretty patterns: rings within rings, the moon and the stars, tiny magpie feet, wild geese flying. Then, with a swift movement of her hand, his mother would make new patterns with tender twigs of pine, reindeer antlers, rippling rays of sunshine, foaming ocean waves, fluffy clouds—all formed from the shells and stones, berries, and blossoms in her three pouches. She also taught her son to make his own patterns, to sing strange, wistful lullabies, and to cut a hollow stem from a reed with which to warble like a blackbird or a nightingale.

Yet as one year blended with the next, the seal-wife changed. Her bright, shining eyes began to fade, her sight grew dim, her soft skin became wrinkled and dry, her thick brown hair turned grey and thin; and her body lost its full, rounded form. Soon she was no more than skin stretched tightly over aching bones.

At long last the seven years had passed and one night she went to the fisherman to claim back her selkie skin. But he would not give it up; he feared that she would return to her ocean home.

Their angry words awoke their little son. In fear, he watched from his bed through half-shut eyes as his father flung open the door of the cottage and strode into the night. The boy loved his mother dearly and was afraid to lose her; softly he cried himself back to sleep.

Next morning, the boy awoke to find his father gone and his mother still asleep. As he stepped out of the cottage, a gust of wind pushed him towards the barn. Stumbling through the door of the barn, he felt a soft blow upon the head—the wind had blown down a bundle that had been lying on a beam.

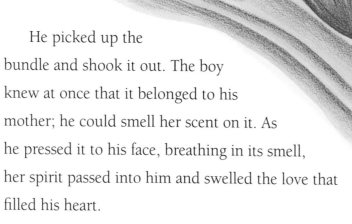

He picked up the
bundle and shook it out. The boy
knew at once that it belonged to his
mother; he could smell her scent on it. As
he pressed it to his face, breathing in its smell,
her spirit passed into him and swelled the love that
filled his heart.

Quickly, he rushed back to the cottage and laid the skin upon his
mother's sleeping form. In an instant she was awake, leaping out of bed
and pulling on the skin.

"Oh, my darling boy," she sighed. "I must away to my own home."

Her words were like a knife in his heart.

"Take me with you, Mother," he said, tears filling his eyes.

She glanced at the beckoning sea, then down at her little son—and
she hesitated. How could she abandon him, her own flesh and blood?

Picking him up, she tucked the boy under her arm and ran across the
heather to the cliff, hurrying down the path towards the beach. Then she

stopped, uncertain what to do next. All at once, taking his face in her hands, she breathed three sweet breaths into his lungs and, clutching her precious bundle, dived into the roaring foam.

They swam together and breathed like two grey seals until they came to an underwater cave, where a whole family of seals was playing, eating, singing, dancing. An old silver seal approached: he greeted the woman seal and her child, calling him "little grandson."

"Welcome home, daughter," he said with a smile. "A bonnie child you bring."

"He must return to his own folk, Father," she said. "His time is not yet come; he cannot stay with us beneath the sea."

She wept. The old seal wept. And the half-seal wept too.

Seven days passed and the mother seal's eyes and hair grew bright, her sight became as keen as ever, her skin was smooth and glossy, and she grew plump and well again.

Now she could swim wild and free, no more a prisoner on the land.

When the time came, the grandfather and mother swam towards the shore with the child between them. And they gently placed him on a rock near his father's home. Before she dropped back into the waves, the mother told her son, "I'll be with you always. Aye, and when you lift your voice to sing, I'll breathe into your lungs a sweet breath of song."

Then she was gone.

The boy grew up to be a great teller of stories and singer of songs. Some said he had the gift of the seal's breath inside him—the spirit of his selkie mother. Sometimes, in the grey mists of dawn or fading dusk, folk would see him kneeling in his boat upon the swell; he seemed to be talking to a seal who often swam near the shore. None dared hunt her, for she was said to be mother to the man and the protector of the earth itself.

Did not her deep eyes say it was so?

# *The Little Mermaid*

*DANISH*

Far, far away, where the waters are as clear as crystal and as blue as cornflowers, dwell the merfolk. You must not think that only sand lies beneath the ocean. There are the strangest plants and trees whose leaves are so light that the slightest motion of the waves makes them sway to and fro. Fish glide through the branches, just as birds fly in and out of trees on land.

Where the sea is deepest stands the palace of the Mer King. Its walls are of coral and its windows of amber; its roof is of oyster shells that open and shut, revealing glittering pearls fit for any earth king's crown.

The Mer King's children were the prettiest little mermaids; and the youngest was the loveliest of all. Her skin was as soft as a rose petal, her eyes were as blue as the deep blue sea; yet, like any mermaid's, her body ended in a tail.

On her fifteenth birthday, this little mermaid was allowed to swim to the surface of the sea and gaze at the world above. Excitedly, she rose as lightly as a speck of foam.

The sun was just setting when she raised her head above the waves. A three-masted schooner lay at anchor nearby. In the growing darkness, hundreds of twinkling lamps swayed in the rigging, lighting up the sea.

The little mermaid swam to a cabin porthole and, every now and then, as the waves lifted her up, she could see within. She saw fine gentlemen inside the boat, the handsomest among them being a young prince with large, dark eyes. A party was being held to celebrate his birthday; and he laughed and joked, shaking hands with everyone.

It was now quite late, yet the little mermaid could not tear her gaze away. Then, all of a sudden, she heard a deep rumbling from the ocean depths and the ship began to roll. A fierce storm was brewing. In next to no time, the schooner was being tossed about on stormy seas; one instant the ship rose aloft, the next it plunged below.

The little mermaid thought this was splendid fun; but the sailors and their passengers were terrified. The ship's planks creaked, the stout masts bent and then, with a terrifying crack, the main mast snapped and the ship rolled over into the sea.

The little mermaid swam through the broken beams and spars, desperately searching for the prince. At last she found him: his eyes were closed, his head barely bobbed above the waves, and it seemed certain that

he would
drown. She
rushed to help
him, holding up his
head as the waves carried
them along.

Towards dawn the storm died down. Not a trace now remained of the
sailing ship. The sun rose warm and bright out of the sea, its rays lending
color to the prince's cheeks. Yet his eyes stayed shut. The little mermaid
kissed his brow and gently brushed the wet hair from his face. She wished
with all her heart that he might live.

In the distance she saw dry land and a church standing at the water's
edge. She swam with the lifeless prince towards the sandy shore, and laid
him on the dry warm sand, taking care to place his head away from the
foaming waves. Then, seeing someone approach, the little mermaid
quickly swam out to some rocks to hide.

A young woman walking along the shore found the prince's body;
quickly she called for help and a host of people came crowding round.
The little mermaid watched as the prince opened his eyes and smiled at
the face before him. How could he know that it was the little mermaid
who had saved his life?

The prince was carried gently to the church. When she could no
longer see him, the little mermaid dived down to her home beneath the
sea. But she could not forget the prince.

Many an evening, she would swim to that sandy shore. She saw the snows on the mountains melt, the fruit in the gardens fall, and the flowers fade and die; yet she never saw the prince again. She was very sad, for she loved him with all her heart. How she wished to be a real woman whom he might love in return!

One day, she asked her grandmother, "Granny, can a mermaid become a woman?"

"There is one way," her grandmother replied. "If a man falls in love with you, then you may become human too. But it is unlikely: to us our lovely fishtails are a precious treasure, but to humans they are ugly and graceless."

The little mermaid sighed, gazing sadly at her tail. She could not forget the handsome prince, and she longed to win his love. So she made up her mind: she would go to the Sea Witch for advice.

Swimming down through the swirling whirlpool below which the Sea Witch dwelt, the little mermaid found herself outside a hut made of drowned sailors' bones. There sat the witch, a slimy toad upon her lap.

"I know why you've come," the Sea Witch said. "You want to exchange your tail for two stumps on which to walk; and you want the

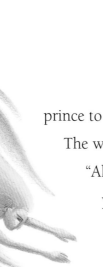

prince to fall in love with you."

The witch gave an evil cackle.

"All right, my dear; I'll mix a potion for
you. Drink it tomorrow before sunrise as
you sit on the shore. Your tail will
divide in two until it becomes what
humans call their 'legs.' But mark my
words: every step you take will be like a sharp knife cutting you to the
bone. And once you have a human body, you can never return to
mermaid form."

"I will do it, no matter how much pain I have to bear," said the
little mermaid.

"Besides all this, I must be paid," the witch added. "Your voice will be
payment for my potion."

"But if you take my voice," the mermaid said, "how will I win the
prince's love?"

"You have your grace, your beauty and your eyes," the witch replied.
"You can capture a man's heart with all of these."

The little mermaid trembled, but her mind was set.

The poor little thing was now struck dumb; she could neither speak
nor sing. Taking the magic potion, she swam back through the whirlpool
to her father's palace and, blowing silent kisses to her sisters, she rose
through the dark blue waters to the world above.

The sun had not yet risen when she reached the prince's realm and sat
down upon the shore. The pale moon still shone above her as she drank

the liquid down; she felt it cut through her body like a knife, and she
fainted clean away. As the sun woke, so did she. At once she felt a burning
fire in all her limbs.

With a sudden gasp she opened her eyes, and there before her stood the prince, his coal-black eyes fixed upon her naked form. Full of shame, she covered herself with her long silken hair and, glancing down, saw that she now had two long, slender legs.

The prince asked her who she was and how she had come ashore. All she could do was smile sadly, gazing at him with her deep blue eyes—for she could not speak a word. Puzzled, the prince took her by the hand and led her to his palace. As the Sea Witch had promised, every step she took was like walking on a knife. But silently she bore the pain. On she went, as graceful as a gazelle, and all who saw her wondered at her beauty.

Rich clothes of muslin and fine silk were brought to dress her and she became the most lovely woman anyone had ever seen. The prince clapped his hands for slave girls to come and entertain her; but none danced as gracefully as she did herself, though every step caused her anguish.

Everyone was enchanted by this mysterious creature, especially the prince. He vowed that she would never leave his side, and he had a velvet couch for her set beside his own. Together they would ride each day through sweet-scented woods, climb misty hills, and bathe in cool springs. At night, the little mermaid would often go to dip her aching feet in the caressing sea; and she would recall her loved ones down below.

Every day, the prince grew fonder of the little mermaid; yet he looked upon her more as a companion than as a wife to love.

"You are more precious to me than all I own," he once said. "You remind me of a woman I once knew. I was on board a ship wrecked by a sudden squall and this woman saved my life. Her alone can I ever love."

He did not know it was the little mermaid who had saved his life.

One day, the prince told the little mermaid, "I must go to visit the daughter of a distant king. My father wishes me to meet this fair princess."

Next morning, they set sail together; on arrival they were taken to the palace to meet the princess. The little mermaid had never seen so beautiful a woman; as for the prince, he stood rooted to the spot.

"It is my long-lost love!" he cried. "You saved my life when I lay half dead upon the shore."

"You must share my joy," he told the little mermaid. "What I dared not hope for has come true."

The little mermaid felt her heart would break.

The happy pair were married at once, with the little mermaid as bridesmaid. That same night, the wedding party sailed smoothly away in the prince's ship.

At midnight, the prince and his bride went below. All was now still. Only the captain and the little mermaid were awake. She stood with her pale arms resting on the rail and gazed eastwards; she no longer wished to live.

All of a sudden, she saw her sisters rising from the sea; their faces were deathly pale and their lovely waist-length hair was gone.

"We have given our hair to the Sea Witch," they said, "so that you will not die. In exchange she gave us a dagger: before sunrise you must plunge it into the prince's heart, and when his warm blood pours out, your blood-washed feet will turn into a fishtail and you will become a mermaid once again. Do it quickly and come home with us."

In a moment they were gone.

The little mermaid went below with the dagger and drew aside the curtains of the bridal couch.

She raised the dagger but, before she could bring it down, she burst into bitter tears: how could she kill the man she loved?

Running from the cabin, she threw the weapon far out to sea.

Then the little mermaid dived into the sea, down, down, down into the watery depths. As she plunged below, her body slowly melted into foam.

When the sun rose, its rays fell warmly upon the white-specked waves and caressed the fading foam—all that remained of the little mermaid's broken heart.

30

# Why the Sea Is Salty

*FINNISH*

At the edge of the forest where fir and larch sweep down to the Baltic Sea, there stands a village of wooden huts. One Christmas, the sound of children crying could be heard from inside one of the huts. It was the home of a poor fisherman who had no food to give his seven children. In despair, his wife sent him to his rich brother's house, at the other end of the village.

When he reached the house, the poor man asked, "Can you give me some food for Christmas, brother? My children are starving."

The rich man thrust a cow's hoof into the poor man's hand, with the words: "Now go to the Devil!"

Away went the poor man with the cow's hoof in his hand
and a frown upon his brow.

"If my brother says so," he mumbled to himself, "I must go to the
Devil. But where will I find him?"

He went into the forest, following a beaten track until he caught the
sound of woodmen at their work.

"Hey, woodmen," he called. "Do you know where the Devil lives?"

"Sure we do," they said. "The Devil is Heesi, master of this forest;
we're his woodcutters."

"How do I reach his house?"

"Follow the trail of felled trees and you'll get there soon enough. But
take our advice: carry with you a birchwood log, for as you enter his
house he'll shake your hand. Give him the log instead or he'll make
mincemeat of your hand. And one thing more. Should he offer you a gift,
ask for nothing save his millstone. He keeps it hanging on the wall. Do
that and you'll never want for food again."

Thanking the woodmen for their advice, the poor man went on his
way until he came to Heesi's house. With a polite knock, he walked in
and stood before a tall stone stove. There on top sat Heesi, his white hair
and beard flowing to the floor, a single yellow tooth hanging over his
bottom lip, his gnarled brown hands broader than the widest tree.

The fisherman stared about him nervously, as Heesi
stretched out his enormous hand and roared,
"Welcome, Guest!"

At once, the poor man thrust his birchwood log into
Heesi's hand—and stared as sawdust ran through the Devil's
fingers to the floor.

"I've brought you a gift," he stuttered. "A cow's hoof."

Old Heesi smiled. Taking the hoof, he crunched it
contentedly with his gums and swallowed it down, not leaving a
scrap of bone.

"Many promise me food," he said, "but none dare come near my
home. Now, what will you have as your reward? Gold, silver?"

"I've no use for either," the poor man said. "But since you offer me
a reward, I'll take the millstone hanging on your wall."

Old Heesi's smile soon faded. He did not want to part with his
millstone; so he offered a pot of gold, a tub of silver, a chest of
salt. But the poor man was as stubborn as he was simple,
and he refused them all.

"Ah, well," Heesi sighed at last, "I suppose I must

grant you what you ask. Take the millstone; you have only to say, 'Grind, my millstone, grind away!' and it will bring you all you wish. And when you've had enough, tell it, 'Stop, my millstone, grind no more!' and it will cease. Now be off before I change my mind."

The fisherman took the millstone and set off for home with it on his

back. As he reached the door of the hut, he saw his angry wife waiting for him, hands on hips.

"Where have you been, you good-for-nothing?" she shouted. "And what's that you're carrying on your back? We can't put a millstone in the pot to boil!"

With a smile, he put the millstone on the
table and shouted loud enough to raise the roof,
"Grind, my millstone, grind away;
Bring plenty of food for the holiday!"
Heesi's millstone at once began to turn
round and round, pouring out loaves of bread
and rings of rolls, jugs of milk and cabbage
pies, salted sprats and rounds of cheese. Never
in their lives had the family set their eyes upon such tasty food. Quickly,
the wife brought sacks and bowls and filled them full of food; and still the
millstone ground away. Finally, the poor man said, "Stop, my millstone,
grind no more!"

While the hungry family were eating their fill, the rich brother chanced
to look in at the door. His eyes grew wide in surprise.

"I see my cow's hoof served you well," he said.

"Yes, indeed, Brother," the poor man replied. "I did exactly as you said
and went to the Devil; and I brought back his millstone. All we have to say
is 'Grind, my millstone, grind away!' and
it brings all we need."

Being jealous of his brother's good
fortune, the rich man was eager to get his
hands on the magic millstone. So he said,
"Lend me the millstone for a while. After
all, it was my cow's hoof that brought
you good luck."

The simple-hearted man readily agreed. However, such was the greedy brother's haste that he didn't wait to hear about the words that stopped the stone.

Hurrying down to the shore, he set the millstone in the bows of his fishing boat and headed out to sea. When he was already far out, he cast his nets into the sea and soon pulled in a heavy catch. Not satisfied with this, he decided to salt the fish without delay. Standing up in his boat, he yelled above the gusting wind,

"Grind, my millstone, grind away;
Pour out salt the livelong day!"

At once, the millstone began to spin and turn, grinding out the purest, whitest salt. There was soon enough to salt the whole boatload of teeming fish. The rich man looked on in glee, rubbing his hands. But the salt continued to stream out.

Soon his
smile turned to an anxious
frown. It was time to call a halt. But
what were the words he should use?
"Cease, my millstone, stop, stop, stop!
Grind no more, no more, no more!
Enough, enough, enough, I say!"
It was no use.

So heavy was the boat by now that it was sinking lower and lower into the water. Soon the sea was coming over the sides and the boat was near to sinking altogether. The rich man tried desperately to throw the millstone overboard. But it was stuck fast and would not move.

As the sea closed over him, he sank with his boat and its load of fish right down to the ocean floor.

And what of the millstone? The folk who dwell upon those shores say that even at the bottom of the ocean it continued to turn and turn and turn. It remains there still, grinding out an endless stream of salt.

That is why, if you have not already guessed, the sea is full of salt.

# Sea Wind

### SENEGALESE

All day long, Sea Wind roams over islands and seas, through forest and plain, driving herds of timid deer towards the waterholes. In all the daylight hours he refreshes plants, uplifts birds and heralds the changing seasons.

Yet of an evening, when he is tired, he folds his wings and sinks down as the red sun sets. He floats below the clouds, hovers for a moment as he chooses a sand dune or a glade, then settles down to rest.

The great bushland knows his secrets; she knows that each night he takes the form of bird or beast so as to slumber undisturbed.

"Hush, Sea Wind is sleeping," she murmurs to one and all.

The green parrot on the wing—that is Sea Wind.

The silver lizard on the moonlit hill—that is him.

Over the Niger at Lake Debo you may see a flight of pink flamingoes on the pale horizon—that is Sea Wind too.

Sometimes he rests close by a village. Then he stretches out tall and handsome, a warrior lying in the grass, slumbering, head cradled on one arm.

One time when Aminata, a maid of Maca, went to fetch fresh water, she found Sea Wind sleeping beneath a tree and she stopped to look at him. She took him for a wayfarer, a stranger from another land. But what a man: the hero of her dreams, the man she had sought since love first stirred in her breast.

Dust mingled with sweat upon his forehead, his body was scarred with scratches and weeping cuts. With gentle, timid hands the girl cleaned his wounds and bathed his face and eyes.

It was a still, starlit night for the meeting of Aminata and the copper-colored stranger. She was so full of love that she did not hear the old fisherman Abbege poling his way back from Gorom, grumbling as he staggered up the path, bent double beneath his bundle of nets and lines.

The old man used to listen out for Sea Wind and talk to him. "Frish, Frish," he would call.

Out of a tree dived a toucan at dawn's first light. The parrot's eyes flushed pink, and the guinea fowl stretched its neck and rushed off in search of seeds. There came a rustling in the trees as all the animals awoke. With a deep sigh, the broad expanse of open country awoke to morning.

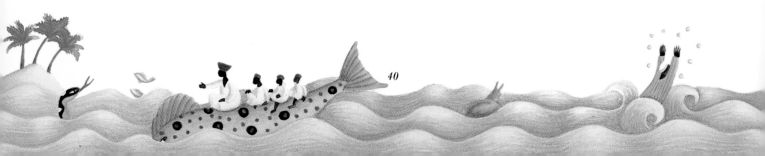

40

Sea Wind opened his eyes. He saw above him a maiden's face, full of tenderness.

"What is your name?" he asked.

"Aminata," the girl replied.

"And who was the first boy in your village to tell you how pretty you are?" She blushed.

"You do not reply, Aminata."

"I like to hear you speak my name," she sighed.

"It is as fresh as the water in your jug," he said.

She lowered her eyes and held out the pitcher for him to drink. He drank deeply.

"I have long awaited a stranger beneath this tree," she murmured. "A man such as you."

For a moment he was silent, then gently he said, "Aminata, in my wanderings I too have dreamed. My dream was of a daughter of the People's tribe who was just like you. But I am a traveller, I never halt; I am from here and there and everywhere where I am not. Yet, somehow I long to stay with you. I grow tired of rushing to and fro about the world."

Before their huts the women pounded millet with their pestles. Abbege unhooked his nets and set off towards the river once again. As he passed by the couple, he was muttering to himself, "Sea Wind is growing old and deaf; he does not hear me."

When he reached the end of the path, they heard him calling—"Frish, Frish"—as he unfurled his

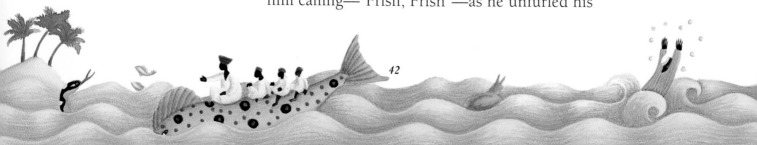

42

patched white sail. Then, all at once, the stranger rose, as light as a butterfly's wing, and gazed into the girl's deep brown eyes, as if making a promise to her.

"Frish is my name," he said softly.

Then, a deep-throated laugh burst from him and his white teeth flashed.

"Well, I must accompany the fisherman to Gorom. He calls my name and I must push him upstream. He thinks I am old and deaf. Oh no, Aminata—Sea Wind is not deaf; he has the sharpest ears."

She did not dare ask when he would return. But he read the unasked question in her eyes.

"I shall return, Aminata. I'll be here this evening beneath the tree."

All day long, her thoughts dwelt on the meeting. When evening came she was there, waiting by the tree.

With the first trembling touch of night he came to her, bending the grass and raising a puff of dust to tickle the house dogs' noses as they sat before the huts, biting and scratching their mangy coats.

Aminata took him home to her family and when her father returned from hunting, they all sat down to eat. Sea Wind ate with his fingers like a man and drank *dolo* beer, made from corn, as he related his adventures. By and by, the elders came to listen to his words.

Voices murmured long into the night in Aminata's hut. For Sea Wind had chosen her to be his wife.

In the passing of the years, Sea Wind and Aminata had two fine children. The first was a boy, Mamadu Marta, which means Sea Breeze; the second a girl, Binetu, which means Flower Wind.

Never were children so lively. In the meadows where the washerwomen spread their linen on the grass to dry, they would run around until they were out of breath; each time they passed they made the clothes swing to and fro.

They would wander into the forest, blowing with all their might into the bushes, putting to flight the partridge, and leading deer astray with their mischievous gusts of wind.

Mamadu Marta would accompany old Abbege to the fishing grounds.

"Frish, Frish," the old fisherman would cry from his *dhow,* a boat with a triangular sail.

And Mamadu Marta would come rushing over the waves, leaping into the *dhow's* stern and blowing the sail fit to tear the canvas.

Binetu learned singing from birds and crickets, and would warble for hours as she walked through fields of flowers, gathering golden sunbeams and scattering them to the breeze. Her breath was fragrant with lilies and orange-blossom. Aminata's garden was full of

44

pretty flowers which her daughter brought from far and near, helping them to flourish with her songs. Her father called the songs "Flowers of the Wind."

It was not often that journeys brought Sea Wind to the village but, when he came, he would stay there for a while. Then Aminata was so happy. He would spend whole nights with her and tell the little ones stories from the lands of the Crimson Sunset.

Throughout those long nights, boats were becalmed upon the sea, dead leaves never fell from branches, and an eerie silence reigned across the world. The earth, water, and grass all found it hard to bear—but no one was troubled at Maca, where it seemed but a short pause before Sea Wind told another story to his children and blew gently upon the embers of the hearth.

For a few years, Sea Wind returned at every change of season. Then, when Aminata gave birth to her third child, he did not come at all.

Aminata was mortally ill after the birth. Her third child was the most handsome of all. He had black eyes and his laughter was like a summer's breeze.

Aminata held him to her breast till her last breath, talking to him as if he understood, hoping for a miracle that would bring back her husband.

Old Abbege said later that towards the dawn he saw a big white seagull pass low over the water, issuing a heart-rending cry and heading for the village. When Abbege went into the village and pushed open Aminata's door, he swore he saw the seagull standing on one leg and gazing at the mother and child.

And as he watched the woman and the bird he heard Aminata say, "You have returned at last, proud nomad of my dreams. Now that you are here, I grieve no more. Farewell, fond Frish—I love you dearly."

The white seagull circled for some moments above the village, then turned and flew straight out to sea.

Sea Wind's third child grew up a sturdy boy. His childhood was that of any normal child, save that he did not play with other children of his age. He preferred to wander by himself, befriending baby birds who had fallen from their nests. He was a lonely boy, yet gentle and kind. The villagers called him Alama, which means Breath of Mercy.

One day, Sea Breeze, Flower Wind, and Breath of Mercy all flew away from their village home.

To Sea Breeze his father gave the realm of oceans, waves, rivers, and swamps. Old Abbege's sons always whistle for him when the kingfisher calls.

The girl, Flower Wind, haunts the fields and woods, and everywhere she goes she brings warm spring days, ripe fruit in autumn and, on hot days, when the air shimmers in the sun, it is she who tosses up those little glittering grains of gold that are neither insect nor flower.

Alama, the last born, has the most beautiful realm of all. He rocks and comforts the sad people of the world, he sings for those who mourn, he brings a breath of joy and a soothing caress to comfort the sick and poor.

# Sinbad the Sailor

EGYPTIAN

In the Golden Age of Haroon Al-Rashid, the Caliph of Baghdad, there lived a wealthy merchant named Sinbad. He had made so many voyages across the sea that everyone called him Sinbad the Sailor.

Once, he set sail from Basrah and crossed the sea, trading everywhere he went. On the voyage home, his ship cast anchor off an island as green and pleasant as the gardens of Paradise. In the company of the crew, Sinbad went ashore to stretch his legs and explore the island. Some of the sailors lit fires to cook food, others washed and scrubbed clean their sea-stained clothing.

All of a sudden, this calm scene was shattered by a shout: "Run for your lives, men! Quick, back to the ship!"

47

The island was moving. A few of the sailors managed to reach the ship. As swiftly as they could they pulled up the anchor and sailed off. But Sinbad and the others were left stranded on the shore as the island heaved and shook, then sank beneath the waves.

What the sailors had taken for an island turned out to be a gigantic whale: it had slept so long in the water that an entire forest had grown upon its back. The whale had been woken by the fires and then dived towards the ocean bed together with all the half-cooked dinners, half-scrubbed clothes, and drowning men.

Sinbad was pitched into the churning sea, where he bobbed up and down amid broken trees and other debris. A washtub floated past his head and, scrambling inside, he paddled furiously with a broken branch to avoid being sucked down into the whirlpool stirred up by the diving whale.

The waves tossed Sinbad about like a piece of flotsam upon the open sea. Night fell and he drifted into fitful sleep. As luck would have it, early the next morning he spotted a sailing ship. With a thumping heart he watched it come toward him; he yelled and yelled until the crew noticed him, steered the ship closer, and plucked him from the waves.

A few days later, the ship put in at an island for fresh water and supplies of food. It was a large island covered with fig and date trees heavy with ripe

fruit. Sinbad went ashore and set out alone; he ate some figs and drank cool water from a clear spring. After a while, he sat down to rest beneath a palm tree and fell asleep.

How long he slept he did not know. But when he awoke the ship had gone, and not a soul remained on shore. His new shipmates had apparently forgotten him in their eagerness to get home.

Sinbad rose slowly to his feet and, to gain a better view of his surroundings, climbed a tree so that he could look in all directions. In the distance, among the trees, a white object caught his eye. He climbed down and made his way towards it, arriving after a short while at a huge oval dome with no doors or windows. Its surface was too smooth to climb and it took Sinbad fifty paces to walk all the way around it.

The day was drawing to a close when suddenly the sky grew dark and a great shadow fell upon the ground. Glancing up, Sinbad saw a huge bird with enormous wings and a beak as long as a sailing ship. At once, he recalled a sailor's tale about monstrous birds called rocs that lived on islands and fed their young on snakes and elephants.

This must be a roc's egg!

As Sinbad hid among the trees, the giant bird flew down and landed on the egg, covering it with its body like a brooding hen.

A desperate plan began to form in Sinbad's mind: perhaps the roc flew to other islands where people lived? Perhaps he would find his way home at last.

Unwinding the turban from his head, he tied one end around his waist and, tiptoeing to the sleeping bird, the other to one of its claws. He waited all night long, holding tight to the bird's claw. At dawn, the bird let out a great squawk and rose into the sky; it did not notice its passenger at all.

Sinbad's heart was in his mouth as he clung to the roc, which soared and swooped across the sea through the morning air. Eventually, it dived down to earth again and landed gently on a rocky plain. Hastily, Sinbad unwound his turban from the roc's claw and, shaking in every limb, ran to safety behind a large boulder. He watched as the bird pounced upon an enormous snake and flew back across the sea with it.

As soon as the bird was gone, he set off to explore the plain. To his dismay, he found that he was in the foothills of a mountain that rose steeply into the sky; it was too high to climb. Before him stretched an endless empty valley, with neither trees, nor pools, nor grass. Not knowing what else to do, Sinbad started walking.

As he made his way across the plain, he was amazed to see that the ground was strewn with diamonds glittering in the sun. Yet it was also covered with hissing snakes, each thicker than a palm tree and big enough to swallow a cow.

Fearing for his life, Sinbad kept close to the mountain wall. But another shock was coming. Right next to him, with a crash, fell the carcass of a sheep. Looking up and shielding his eyes against the sun, he tried to see where the sheep had fallen from.

Then Sinbad remembered a story he had heard long ago about a diamond valley guarded by hordes of snakes. Hunters would toss fresh meat down the mountainside, hoping that some diamonds would stick to the meat. If they were lucky, vultures would then swoop down upon the meat and fly with it to the mountain top, where the hunters would be waiting with bells and drums to scare them off, leaving the meat behind. That way they could take the diamonds for themselves.

This gave Sinbad an idea.

Filling his pockets with as many diamonds as he could, he crawled beneath the sheep and clung tightly to its fleece. After what seemed like a century, he heard the flapping of wings and felt himself being lifted up to the mountain top, where he was dropped with a bump upon the ground. All at once, he heard the most dreadful racket—a clanging, clattering, booming of bells and drums. This soon frightened off the hungry bird.

Imagine the fright Sinbad gave the hunters when they came to claim their prize. Quickly he told his story and shared

the diamonds with the men. In return, they led him safely to a busy port where he joined a ship for Basrah.

But poor Sinbad must have brought bad luck with him wherever he went. Not long after setting sail, the new ship keeled over in a storm and went to the bottom of the sea with all its crew. Once more, good fortune saved Sinbad from a watery grave. Clinging to a spar, he was tossed by wind and waves to another faraway island.

When he came to, Sinbad set out to explore his surroundings. He had not gone far when, to his surprise, he saw an old man sitting beside a stream. He was an odd old fellow with straggly hair and a long white tangled beard, carrying a stick, and naked but for a skirt of banana leaves.

"Hey there, shipmate!" Sinbad called. "How did you come here?"

But the old man said nothing. Instead, he signaled to Sinbad to carry him across the stream. Mindful of the place reserved in heaven for those who help the poor and needy, Sinbad took the fellow upon his shoulders and waded through the stream to the other side.

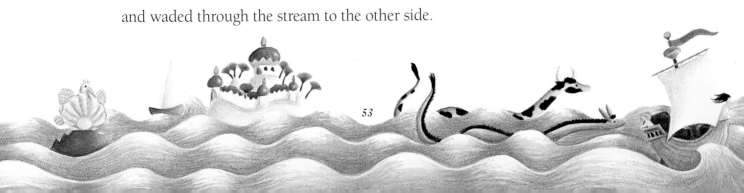

Yet when he tried to set the old man down, he found he would not budge. The fellow twisted his legs around Sinbad's neck and, each time Sinbad tried to throw him off, squeezed so hard on Sinbad's throat that he could not breathe.

So Sinbad had to go wherever the old man wished him to; and if he stopped to catch his breath, the old man beat him black and blue.

So it went on for days and weeks and months, until one day Sinbad reached a glade where vines and pumpkins grew. As the old man slept, Sinbad picked as many branches of fat, juicy grapes as he could find. Then he chose a pumpkin that was big and dry, cleaned it out and filled it with the juice he squeezed from the grapes. After this, he left the pumpkin in the sun for several hours until the juice had turned to wine.

When the old man opened his eyes, Sinbad offered him the drink "to freshen his heart and give him strength." To show the man its power, Sinbad drank deeply from the wine and started to dance.

When the old man saw this, he greedily drained the pumpkin dry. In no time at all, his eyes began to roll, his arms flapped at

his sides, and his legs loosened their grip. Sinbad seized his chance: with a sudden tilt forwards, he sent the old man crashing to the ground, where he lay in a drunken sleep.

Sinbad could scarcely believe his luck. He ran about the island, eating sweet fruit and drinking from the streams, keeping constant watch for a passing ship. One stormy day, when he had almost given up all hope, he

suddenly spied a ship being tossed about
on the angry sea. It had to take refuge in the
bay of the island until the storm passed.
So Sinbad was saved again.

When he told his story, the captain said, "You are a very
lucky man. That old fellow who rode upon your back was the Old Man of
the Sea. He is much feared by mariners—no shipwrecked sailor has ever
escaped from him before."

Several weeks later, Sinbad arrived back home at last. He set
off with an anxious heart to find his family. Were they still
alive? Would they remember him?

He needn't have feared. His children were all
grown up, but his dear wife was overjoyed to see
him again. Sinbad told her his amazing tale and it
was passed from mouth to mouth until it reached
the ears of the Caliph himself. The Caliph
was so impressed that he summoned
Sinbad to his palace and had the story
written down for all to hear.

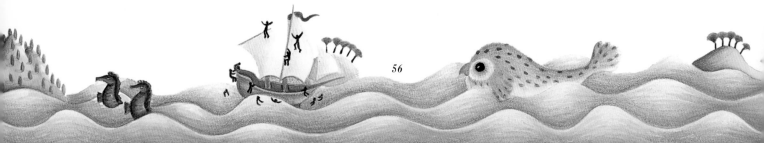

# H i n e - m o a

**MAORI**

At Owhata, on the banks of Lake Rotorua, lived a lovely young woman whose name was Hine-moa. She was strong-limbed and graceful, the pride of her mother, Hine-maru, and her father, Umi-karia. As Umi-karia was a great chief, only the noblest of men could hope to marry his daughter.

In the center of Lake Rotorua lay the island of Mokoia, the home of a young man called Tutanekai. Since the tribes of Hine-moa and Tutanekai were at peace, their people would often visit one another. That was how the young man and the young woman met.

One day, the young men of Mokoia prepared to row across to Owhata to take part in ritual war dances called *hakas,* and ceremonial games.

Before setting off, they gathered presents for the girls of Owhata: sweet herbs and scents and the ripe fruit of the *miro* tree to make fragrant oil.

When they arrived a great crowd had assembled to watch, and the dancers lined up in ranks. First came the steady stamping of the Owhata men. Behind them, led by Hine-moa, came the women, their eyes wide and their bodies swaying in a dance of welcome.

As he watched Hine-moa, Tutanekai's heart beat faster and he knew he would never love another. As if to tease him, Hine-moa jumped up and down, poking out her tongue, then hiding behind the other dancing girls. In that brief moment, love flared up between them though no word was spoken, for they were young and shy.

In the weeks that followed, Tutanekai built himself a hut high up on the hillside of Mokoia, so that he could gaze across the lake. In the cool of

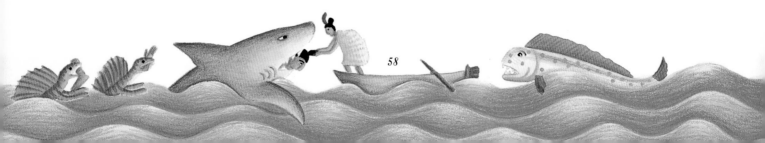

the evening he would sit and play his flute, and sometimes, when the
wind was right, the notes would float on the breeze to the ears of Hine-
moa, making her heart pound.

The young man was too timid to declare his love. Yet after he had met
her at several *hakas,* he became bold enough to press her hand and felt a
warm response from hers. At last, unable to bear his love in silence any

longer, he sent a messenger—such was the custom in those
days—to tell her of his love.

When Hine-moa heard the news, she blushed and
sent her reply: "Tell Tutanekai that our love is one."

After that, Hine-moa could detect a note of
longing in the music that drifted on the evening
breeze across the lake.

Just after sundown one night, at the meeting-house on Mokoia, the young men of the tribe began to talk of Hine-moa.

"Has anyone proof of Hine-moa's love?" one asked.

"I have," cried several youths at once, claiming they had squeezed her hand.

Tutanekai kept silent.

At last, someone asked him too, and he could not tell a lie.

"I have pressed her hand and felt the pressure of hers on mine," he said. "And I have seen the glow of love in her dark eyes."

The young men all laughed.

Tutanekai's eyes filled with tears.

"I know she loves me," he cried. "She said she hears my flute across the lake and knows it plays the song of love. One day, she said, she'll paddle her canoe to join me over here."

"Well, where is she then?" the others jeered. "We hear your love notes every night, but we've never seen her canoe!"

Long into the night they teased him; and he wished he had kept silent.

Meanwhile, back at Owhata, Umi-karia had noticed his daughter's love-sick face whenever the flute was heard across the water. So he

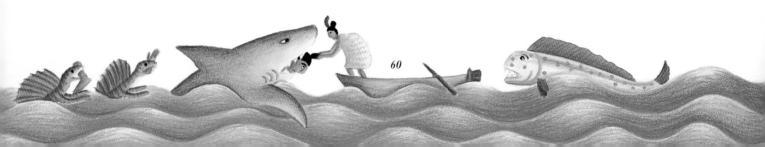

dragged all the canoes well up the beach; Hine-moa could not possibly move them by herself.

What was she to do?

As she stood at the lakeside, listening to the love song from across the water, she felt as if the spirit of the lake was telling her what to do: she should swim to her beloved Tutanekai.

It was a long way from Owhata to Mokoia, but in the lonely sadness of the night, Hine-moa decided to attempt the crossing. She slipped off her clothes and tied six dried gourds around her, three on one side, three on the other; these would help her keep afloat.

Then she dived into Rotorua's dark, cold waters.

There was no moon that night, so no one saw her go; but neither could she see her way. She hoped that Tutanekai's flute would guide her safely through the waves, but no sound came. For what seemed like hours, she battled through the waters until her aching arms and legs could barely carry her forward. Then, just as she thought she would drown, she came upon a tree stump—known today as Hine-whata—sticking out of the water.

Hine-moa clung to it, trying to regain her strength. But the cold water chilled her to the bone, making her too weak to swim on.

All of a sudden, the music of the flute rose up

like a flame, bringing her fresh hope and strength. Weak as she was, she managed to swim on again until at last she felt firm rock beneath her feet. At that moment, the music stopped. It was late, and Tutanekai wanted to sleep.

Down on the beach, below his hut, there was a warm-water pool, now known as Hine-moa's Pool. Shivering with cold, Hine-moa sank her weary body into its warming balm.

After a while, she heard footsteps on the sand. It was Tutanekai's brother, come to fill his *calabash* gourd with water. As he bent down over the pool, he heard a voice in the darkness that almost scared him to death.

"Tell Tutanekai to come here now."

Terrified, the brother ran back to tell Tutanekai of the spirit hidden in the pool. The young man came running at once, wielding a stick and shouting, "Come out, so I can see you!"

When Hine-moa heard her loved one's voice, she hid under some rocks overhanging the pool. Her heart was beating fast and she longed to take him in her arms; but she was too shy. Tutanekai, meanwhile, was feeling his way around the pool when he touched a hand.

"Ah-ha, caught you!" he cried. "Now come out, so I can see you."

Hine-moa stepped from the pool and stood before him, trembling.

"It is I, Hine-moa," she softly said.

Tutanekai could not believe his ears. But as they embraced, her fast-beating heart told him it was indeed his own true love. Wrapping Hine-moa in his cloak, he led her home.

Next morning, as the men of Mokoia sat at breakfast, they suddenly noticed that Tutanekai was missing.

"He must have overslept," said one. "I'll go and fetch him."

He soon returned, with a look of astonishment on his face.

"He's with Hine-moa!" he cried.

"Impossible," the others said. "How could she have crossed the lake alone?"

Then all eyes turned to the hillside as Hine-moa made her way down. Even the few jealous cries were drowned by a roar of welcome from the Mokoia men. No one had ever swum across the lake before; yet this bold young woman had done it all alone, in the dark of the night, for the sake of the man she loved.

Since Hine-moa had crossed the waters in such a strong demonstration of her love, her family now welcomed Tutanekai, and the two tribes were bound more firmly in friendship than before.

Hine-Moa and Tutenakai lived for many years and their love was so great that it has never been forgotten by the Maori people. Today, as the waves break and roll upon the shores of Lake Rotorua, the local people say that they are really Hine-Moa and Tutenakai, who are as inseperable as wave from water. Hine-Moa is now known as the Ocean Maid, while her husband is the Guardian of the Sea. Together, they rule the waters of the oceans, lakes, and streams that wash the earth and protect any voyagers who honor their story.

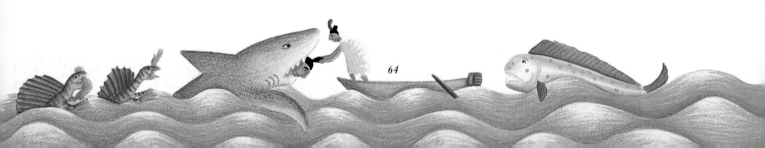

# The Precious Pearl

## VIETNAMESE

Once upon a time there was an orphan girl called Wa who lived beside the China Sea. As soon as she was strong enough to carry a basket of rice upon her back, she started to work for the village headman.

Like the other villagers, she toiled long and hard for her master: she had to cut down the tallest trees and, when the rice was ripe in the paddyfields, she had to peel husks from dawn to dusk. Her hands grew raw from cutting wood, and her palms itched from handling the coarse rice husks.

Each night, she would gather herbs to soothe her itching hands; and her friends would come to her for help, for she had great knowledge of wild plants.

One day, as she
was cleaning the new harvest of rice,
the master came to tell her to guard the rice storehouse,
which stood on stilts close to the sea. The storehouse was filled to the roof
with rice, and the hungry girl longed to eat some. But she remembered
what the master once told her: "An evil spirit protects my rice. If you eat a
single grain, the spirit will leap inside you. Then you will turn into a grain
of rice yourself!"

As darkness fell, Wa grew so tired she fell asleep; but at dawn next
day she was rudely awakened by several hard kicks. It was her master.

"You lazy girl!" he screamed. "Fill this pail with water by the time
I return."

Wa jumped up in alarm as he went laughing unpleasantly on his way.
She took the pail and ran swiftly down to the sea.

The waters were ruffled by a gentle breeze as they lapped softly at the
girl's sore, aching feet. She sighed and bent down to fill the pail. All at
once, the sea began to boil and boom like the strings of a musical
instrument called a *torong*. The noise made her dart back in alarm.

Then out of the foam appeared a woman, tall and proud, wearing a
long green dress. As she approached, she took Wa's trembling hand and
said, "The Sea Spirit's daughter has fallen ill. You know the healing herbs,

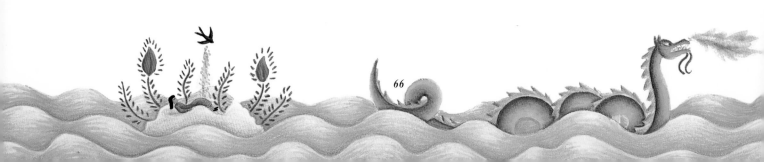

66

so come with me and see the girl."

"No, no, I cannot," Wa cried out. "I have to guard the master's rice."

"The Sea Spirit is mightier than your village chief," the woman said. "If you do not come, the spirits will punish you."

A dry pathway suddenly opened before her in the waves, and the tall young woman led Wa down into the watery depths.

A scorpion had stung the Sea Spirit's daughter while she played upon the shore. All the underwater doctors—the shrimps and eels—were now fussing about the poor sick girl; yet none could help her. For three whole months she had been sick, unable to eat or sleep.

Wa gently examined the wound and told the spirits what herbs to bring. When these were ready, she used them on the girl, and three days later she was well again.

The Sea Spirit was overjoyed.

"Dear Wa," he said, "what will be your reward?"

"I wish only to save my people from need," the girl replied.

Thereupon the Sea Spirit handed her a precious pearl, saying, "Ask the pearl whatever you desire and it will make your wish come true."

Wa thanked the Sea Spirit and returned to the shore along the underwater path. When she reached the rice storehouse, however, she saw bird tracks all around—storks had eaten half the rice!

An old man passing by stared hard at Wa.

"Where have you been for the past three months?" he cried. "Just look at this: those birds have stolen the master's rice. He is searching all over for you, and he's in a towering rage."

Wa continued sadly on her way. Eventually, she sat down upon the ground, hung her head and cried. Her thin dress became quite wet with tears. And then, all at once, she recalled the precious pearl. Taking it out, she murmured, "Pearl, precious pearl, bring me some food."

Right away, a huge bamboo dish appeared, filled with all kinds of tasty food. And at her back a storehouse of rice rose up, three times taller than her master's.

She clapped her hands with joy and feasted to her heart's content.

Next morning, Wa made her way to the headman's house. As soon as he set eyes on the girl, he roared like a stricken ox, "Ahrr-rrr, here comes that lump of cow dung, the one who stole my rice. I'll have you fed to the tigers in the hills!"

"It was not my fault you lost your rice," Wa said. "No matter, I'll make up what you lost; just come to collect it."

"Lead on," he snarled. "I'll take it now. And if what you give me falls short by a single grain, I'll bring your head back on a tray!"

When the headman set eyes upon Wa's rice storehouse, his mouth dropped open in surprise.

"Take the rice I owe you and go," Wa boldly said.

Slowly, the headman made his way back home, both astonished and angry at what he had seen. In a rage, he called his guards.

"Gather up your spears," he yelled. "We'll deal with that low-born girl and take all her rice for ourselves."

But the good people of the village ran swiftly to warn Wa of the master's plan. At once, she took out the

precious pearl and said, "Pearl, precious pearl, protect us from the evil man."

Suddenly, lofty mountains sprang up around the headman's house. Although his men tried to scale the peaks, they could climb no higher than the rocky hills; so, three months later, they had to return to their narrow valley on the plain.

Meanwhile, on the other side of the mountain, the wise and just Wa shared among her friends the wealth the pearl had brought her. The poor people never went hungry again, thanks to the Sea Spirit's precious pearl.

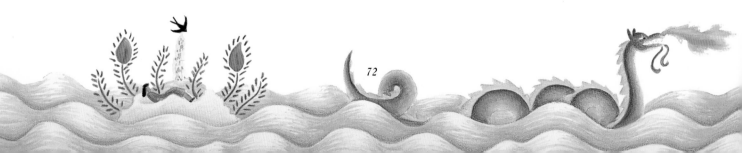

# *The Old Man of the Sea*

SIBERIAN

*I*n times gone by, there stood a camp upon the Amur River's shore. When fish were plentiful, the people sang songs and filled their bellies to the brim. But when the fish were scarce, the people sat sad and silent, smoking pipes of moss and starving in their tents.

So it was one spring. No fish swam in the river and the stores were almost gone. At last, a bold young man, Azmun, spoke out, "I will go to the Old Man of the Sea and ask him to send us fish."

Taking his mouth harp and his fishing line, he walked towards the sun. On and on he went, following the Amur's course, until he arrived at Lia-ari, the Little Sea. Seagulls

73

circled overhead, waves crashed upon the shore, and all around him hungry birds were dying from lack of food.

All of a sudden, he caught the sound of men talking nearby. As he watched from behind a rock, he saw a group of youths, looking fit and well and not at all hungry as they held sword fights upon the strand.

After a while, the young men grew tired and, leaving their swords upon the sand, went off to take a rest by their boats. No one noticed Azmun as he hooked his fishing line round one sword and pulled it towards him.

When the youths returned to gather up their swords, one found his missing.

"Hoya, hoya!" he shouted. "The Old Man will be mad; I cannot return without my sword."

Azmun lay stock still behind his rock as they searched for the missing sword; but after a time, they gave up and went to board their boats. In haste, Azmun ran down the beach, seized an empty boat, and, pushing it into the water, sailed quickly after the other men. Yet all at once, they disappeared. All Azmun could see was a school of little whales, swimming before him, the fins on their backs parting the waves like swords. As he gazed in wonder, he felt his boat rock beneath him; looking down, he saw that he was riding on a whale, though this one had no fin.

Of course! he realized. The youths playing on the shore were little whales, and the swords in their hands were their fins!

He could already see, in the distance, an island rising from the sea

like the roof of a giant tent, with smoke curling upwards from its peak.
As Azmun's whale approached the shore, it rolled over on to its back,
tossing him into the sea: it was afraid to face the Old Man without
its sword.

    As soon as the other whales reached the island, they changed back
into men. When they had disappeared, Azmun swam ashore and made
for the hilltop from which the smoke emerged; and there he found a
chimney, just like the smoke-hole of a tent.

    Hooking his fishing line against the top of the chimney, Azmun

climbed through it—dropping right into the Old Man's tent, or *yaranga*.

Landing on the floor, he glanced about him and was surprised to find the *yaranga* was like that of any man, with a plank bed, earthen floor, embers on the hearth, walls of walrus skin, and a tent pole. But everything was giant-sized and draped in seaweed and shells. On the plank bed lay the Old Man, fast asleep, his green wavy hair spread like seaweed around his head. From the corner of his mouth poked a giant pipe, puffing grey-green clouds of smoke up through the chimney.

Even when Azmun shook him by the shoulder, the Old Man did not wake up. Then the young man thought of his mouth harp—his *kungakay*. So he took it from his bag, fitted it between his teeth and began to play. The *kungakay* hummed and sighed, and gave out music as if the birds were singing in the trees, as if the waters were babbling in the brooks, as if the bees were buzzing in the hives.

The Old Man had never heard anything like it.

He sat up, rubbed his eyes, and set his bare feet on the floor, towering over Azmun like a cliff above the sands.

Seeing the tiny fellow before him, like a sprat before a whale, and hearing the sweet music, the Old Man asked, "Why have you come to my island in the sea?"

Azmun told of the starving people and hungry creatures on the land.

"If you don't send us fish, we will surely die."

"Dear me," muttered the Old Man. "And all because I overslept. How

glad I am you came."

With that he reached beneath the bed
and pulled out a giant pot. All kinds of fish swam
in it: trout and salmon, carp and pike, sprat and cod,
tiny minnows and mighty marlin. A whale skin lay beside the
pot and the Old Man filled it with fish. Then, opening a trap-door
in the floor, he poured the fish into the sea, shouting, "Off you go.
Swim up the Amur and give the people a splendid catch."

Reaching under the bed a second time, the Old Man brought out
another, smaller pot, full to the brim with salted herring. This he offered to
Azmun for the hungry youth to eat his fill.

Azmun was overjoyed.

"How can I repay your kindness?" he said. "All I have is my *kungakay*;
pray, take it—it is yours."

The young man handed the giant his mouth harp and showed him how
to play different tunes. Then he thanked the Old Man again, climbed back
up the chimney and out into the light of day. He glanced happily about
him and saw the little whales chasing fish towards the shore.

But how was he to reach home? Looking around, he noticed a rainbow.
One end was on the island, the other touched a distant shore. Azmun
climbed up and up; the path was very slippery, yet he pulled himself to the
very top, then slid down the other side. Gazing about him on the sand, he
saw the poor whale-youth wandering around, still searching for his sword.
Azmun handed it to him.

"Oh, thank you," said the whale-youth. "For your kindness, I'll drive

78

the fish right up the river to your
camp."

Meanwhile Azmun made his way along the
riverbank until he reached the camp. His people were
sitting on the shore, their eyes dim, their gaunt cheeks
sunken into sallow jaws, their bellies bloated with hunger.

Azmun's father came walking wearily from his *yaranga* to
greet his son, sniffing his neck fondly.

"Did you find the Old Man of the Sea, my son?" he croaked.

"Just look into the river, Father," said Azmun in reply.

The river was teeming with fish of every kind. When Azmun hurled his
harpoon into the water, he speared a dozen at once.

"Is that enough fish, Father?" asked the young man.

"It is, my son," said the old man with a smile.

From that day on, the people had plenty of fish to
eat all through the year. Now, when the sea is restless
and waves lash the cliffs, when the people hear the
white crests hiss above the waves, and the seagulls
shriek in the howling gale, they do not worry. For
they know it is really the Old Man of the
Sea playing his *kungakay*, dancing in his
tent beneath the waves to keep himself
awake, and stirring up a storm.

# Sources

"The Flood" is a Squamish tale from British Columbia, based here on the version given by the half-Mohawk, half-English Emily Pauline Johnson in her *Legends of Vancouver* (Toronto, 1961).

"The Selkie Wife" is from Orkney in the north of Scotland. The version in this book is based on "The Goodman of Wastness" in W. Traill Dennison's *Scottish Antiquary* VII (1892) and G. F. Black's *Country Folk-lore* III (1903), in which the tale was recorded from a native of Ronaldsay.

"The Little Mermaid" is abridged from the tale in the collection of stories by the Danish author Hans Christian Andersen (1805–75).

"Why the Sea is Salty" appears in many folklore collections. The story comes from Karelia and is common to all Finnish peoples, including the Estonians and Karelians. This version is translated from the collection edited by U. S. Konkka, *Karelskie skazki* (*Karelian Fairy Tales*—Petrozavoksk, 1977).

"Sea Wind" is a story from Senegal in Africa, adapted here from the version in René Guillot's *Nouveaux Contes d'Afrique* (*New Tales from Africa*—Paris, 1963).

"Sinbad the Sailor" is based on versions of the tale in Edward William Lane's *The Thousand and One Nights* (London, 1883); Andrew Lang's *Arabian Nights* (London, 1898); Sir Richard Burton's *The Arabian Nights' Entertainments* (London, 1954); and my *Tales from the Arabian Nights* (London, 1983). All these versions of the story were derived from an Egyptian text, probably of fourteenth- or fifteenth-century origin.

"Hine-moa" is a Maori story from New Zealand; this version is based on A. W. Reed's *Wonder Tales of Maoriland* (Wellington, 1964) and Kiri Te Kanawa's *Land of the Long White Cloud: Maori Myths, Tales and Legends* (London, 1989).

"The Precious Pearl" is from Vietnam, translated from Claire Demange's *Contes d'Indochine* (*Stories from Indochina*—Paris, 1980).

"The Old Man of the Sea" is a Nivkh tale from northeastern Siberia. Here it is translated from the version given in M. Voskoboinikov's *Yazyki i folklor narodov krainevo severa* (*Languages and Folklore of the Peoples of the Far North*—Leningrad, 1959). The story is also contained in my *The Sun Maiden and the Crescent Moon: Siberian Folk Tales* (Edinburgh, 1989).